Resurrection Multiplication

Miracle Production

■ ■ ■

Volume 5 in the
Success Series

By Prince Handley

University of Excellence Press

Copyright © 2009 by Prince Handley
All Rights Reserved.

UNIVERSITY OF EXCELLENCE PRESS
Los Angeles ■ London ■ Tel Aviv

ISBN-13: 978-0692340509
ISBN-10: 0692340505

First Edition

✚

The only Resurrection book you need!

TABLE OF CONTENTS

Foreword

Experience resurrection – die to sleep

Experience resurrection – die to bills

Experience resurrection – die to rain

Experience resurrection – die to comfort zones

Experience resurrection – die to automobiles

Experience resurrection – die to ministry

Experience resurrection – die to reasoning

Bonus Resources to help you on your way

FOREWORD

The reason I wrote this book is so **you can experience MIRACLES of resurrection**. This book's *Table of Contents*—unless you read the book—will make NO sense to you.

WARNING: If you read this book it will completely revolutionize your life. If you dare to follow the principles laid out in this book you will experience **quantum leaps of miracle productivity** in your life ... and in your business or service for God.

You'll have to be a Holy Spirit gambler ... and be willing to try! However, the cards are "marked" and the game is "fixed" ... in your favor. If you're playing against Satan you can "call his bluff" because **YOU have the best hand:** it is your Father's hand.

To help you—and to build your confidence to try—I am going to **provide you with personal examples** in my life! After all, the greatest Jew alive today died and was resurrected. If you know Him—and you can—WHY would this principle of **Death and Resurrection** NOT work in your life?!

Hang on! It's a bumpy ride, but you will enjoy the bumps!

Prince Handley

Resurrection Multiplication

Miracle Production

■ ■ ■

EXPERIENCE RESURRECTION

DIE TO SLEEP

Jesus taught, *"Except a grain of wheat falls into the ground and die, it abides alone: but if it die, it brings forth much fruit."* (John 12:24)

What is it that God is asking YOU to DIE TO at this point of your life, ministry, business, or family?

If YOU will DIE to that thing, or to those things, about which God is speaking TO YOU, you will see resurrection: MIRACLE production!

One time God told me to **die to my sleep**. (At that time that was meddling ... a real death!) I promised God I would do this, and in a few days God gave me the opportunity to prove my sincerity!!

One morning I was sleeping soundly and the Lord prompted me to get up early to go to a prayer meeting scheduled for 6:00 AM. **I did NOT want to get up** because I was sleeping soundly (the kind of sleep where you wake up and smile because you don't have to get up!). Also, I just did NOT want to go to the prayer meeting. However, I remembered my promise to God, and grudgingly arose and went to shower. My body did not want to go to the prayer meeting. My mind did not want to go to the prayer meeting. I did not want to go to the prayer meeting!

When I arrived at the prayer meeting there were only a few men there. As I was about to enter the door a man grabbed my hand to shake it and left something in the palm of my hand. **When I opened my hand to look I saw lots of hundred dollar bills**. I woke up real fast. I was so glad I went to the prayer meeting: **my body was glad ... my mind was glad ... and I was glad; we were all glad!**

The person who put the money in my hand did NOT know that I had an important foreign language project I was working on and that money allowed me to sow into the field of many countries. As God is my witness, I can account for every dollar being used for that project (except for I think 26 cents). Multiplied thousands of people have been reached for Messiah Jesus and built up as disciples for many years as a result.

I died to my sleep and God brought resurrection power – MIRACLE harvests – to many nations, tribes, and people!

What is God asking YOU to DIE TO? Is it that power play in your family or at the office, is it your impatience or your ego, OR is it that interpersonal relationship at your church or ministry? What is it about which the LORD is ... or has been ... dealing with you? Is it a person or thing? I promise you on the authority of God's Holy Word that if YOU will DIE to that, God will bring forth resurrection life!

Pray NOW ... obey God, and yield to Him. **Die to that situation, person, or thing ... and then watch God bring resurrection life and multiply it around the world!**

EXPERIENCE RESURRECTION
DIE TO BILLS

Jesus taught, *"Except a grain of wheat falls into the ground and die, it abides alone: but if it die, it brings forth much fruit."* (John 12:24)

What is it that God is asking YOU to DIE TO at this point of your life and ministry?

If YOU will DIE to that thing, or to those things, about which God is speaking TO YOU, you will see resurrection!

One time God told me to die **to my phone bill**. (Before mobile phones I had phone bills as high as $900 a month.) **He told me that if He desired for me to call someone and prophesy to them, even to another country, that I should obey ... and NOT to worry about the phone bill**. I promised God I would do this, and in a few days God, as usual, gave me an opportunity to prove my sincerity!!

While at a restaurant with some people I had just met, I overheard one of them talk about a minister who had been in an automobile wreck a few days before. The man's wife had died in the accident and the minister was still in a coma. He had been a youth minister at the local church years before and nobody knew how to contact him, except that he was about 2,000 miles away in the Twin Cities area (USA).

A few days later, while I was my bedroom praying on my knees, God spoke to my heart, and said: **"Call that minister and prophesy to him."** I thought, *"Is this God or the devil?"* I also thought, *"I don't even know where he's at!"* **But then I had another thought which has enabled me to SEE lots of MIRACLES through the years since:** I thought, **"At least I could give God the benefit of the doubt ... and try!"**

As I was getting off my knees to go call (wherever he was at), **the Lord spoke to me again**, and said, *"You received a letter from your mother last week that your aunt was in the hospital. **Call her on the telephone and pray for her out loud (aloud) in tongues and I will heal her.**"* I thought, *"I don't know where she's at either, but it shouldn't be too hard to find her as there are only two hospitals in the city where she lives."*

THE MINISTER I CALLED

When I called to find the minister it only took me two calls to find the hospital where he was a patient. I was able to call into his room. He was out of the coma; I **prophesied to him, read him a Psalm, and then ended the call. Nobody knew about this!**

About two days later I was invited to speak on Sunday morning at a large business and professional Sunday

School class at the First Baptist Church. One of the leaders of the class, Leon Brooks, was a Messianic Jew. Because the class had been studying "**Motivation**" he asked me to come speak on "**The Gifts of the Holy Spirit**." That next Sunday morning, as I was seated in the class getting ready to speak, I prayed and asked God to open the door for me to share effectively on the gifts.

While sitting there one of the leaders told the people, *"Last week a minister who was on staff here several years ago was in an auto wreck; his wife was killed (and I think children) and he is still in a coma, but we don't know where he's at."* Immediately I thought, *"There's my open door!"* But I forgot about it when I got up to teach.

While I was teaching on the various gifts of the Spirit, as I came to the "**gift of prophecy**", I suddenly remembered about the minister: the one to whom God told me: *"Call that minister and prophesy to him."* I related the experience to the people in the large class and, as I wrote on the chalk board, told them: ***"If you would like to contact him [the minister], he's in Ramsey Hospital, Room 650, Bed #2, St. Paul, Minnesota."***

When I turned around it was as though the whole large gathering of Baptist business people was going to explode. A few minutes later a lady said: ***"Fire is going through my body,"**** and she was miraculously healed**. Several were healed that day.

10

The next week I was invited by one of the elder/deacons to come teach at his home. He told me, *"We want to see God's spirit manifest Himself again!"*

The night I spoke at the elder/deacon's home several were baptized in the Holy Spirit and spoke in tongues. **The next Sunday 125 people were saved at the First Baptist Church. I had died to my phone bill and God brought resurrection power!**

About two or three years later I was ministering to a ladies group in a distant area, and while speaking the Holy Spirit prompted me to tell about the incident described above. I had never mentioned the minister's name before but the Holy Spirit instructed me: ***"Tell them the minister's name."*** I said to the women, *"The minister's name is Mark Shore."* After the meeting a lady rushed up to me and said, *"You haven't heard the rest of this story!"*

The lady told me, *"As a result of the prophecy you gave that minister after he came out of the coma, his mother-in-law was saved and she now travels and speaks to large groups of women internationally."* The lady also told me, *"I just heard her speak recently!"*

I died to my phone bill and God brought wholeness and resurrection power to a minister and his mother-in-law and then multiplied it around the world!

What is it that God is asking YOU to DIE TO at this point of your life and ministry?

If YOU will DIE to that thing, or to those things, about which God is speaking TO YOU, you will see resurrection!

MY AUNT I CALLED

When I phoned to pray for my aunt I found her at the first hospital I called. My aunt was to have surgery the next day. I did NOT ask her what was wrong with her. I **just prayed for her aloud in tongues – in the Spirit – as God had instructed me. I said *"Goodbye"* and hung up the phone.**

Somewhere between six and nine months later I was traveling about 2,500 miles away from home by automobile and was near where my aunt lived. I had NOT seen her in years and decided to visit. I arrived with NO notice, and at that time **a lady from another state was visiting my aunt**; the lady was a distant cousin to her, but not related to me.

This same lady was at the hospital visiting my aunt when I phoned her months before. She told me: *"Your aunt had an abdominal cancer the size of a fist and was swelled up. **When you prayed in tongues for her she was instantly healed and the swelling reduced immediately**. She was healed by the MIRACLE working power of the Holy Spirit and did NOT have to have surgery the next day!"*

12

I died to my phone bill and God brought healing to my aunt!

What is it that God is asking YOU to DIE TO at this point of your life and ministry?

If YOU will DIE to that thing, or to those things, about which God is speaking TO YOU, you will see resurrection power come forth and then multiply around the world!!!

It's up to you ... the ball is in your court.

What is God asking YOU to DIE TO? Is it that power play in your family or at the office, is it your impatience or your ego, OR is it that interpersonal relationship at your synagogue, your church or your ministry? What is it about which the Lord is ... or has been ... dealing with you? Is it a person or thing? God will never deny you anything ... or anyone ... except to give you something else, or someone else, better!

I promise you on the authority of God's Holy Word that if YOU will DIE to that, God will bring forth resurrection life!

Pray NOW ... obey God, and yield to Him. Die to that situation, person, or thing ... and then watch God bring resurrection life and multiply it around the world!

EXPERIENCE RESURRECTION
DIE TO RAIN

Jesus taught, *"Except a grain of wheat falls into the ground and die, it abides alone: but if it die, it brings forth much fruit."* [John 12:24]

If YOU will DIE to that thing, or to those things, about which God is speaking TO YOU, you will see resurrection!

One day God spoke to me to go preach in the open air in a large metropolitan area **during a torrential downpour of rain**. I thought, *"I only have one suit ... and one pair of dress shoes!"* I would always wear a suit and tie when I preached.

It was raining so heavily for such a long period of time that the water was coming over the curb onto the sidewalk. People were actually taking off their shoes and carrying them across the streets.

I was not using a loudspeaker or amplification equipment, just preaching into the loud rain with my voice to the passersby. **On the way home my good black shoes were turning white, my suit was drenched, and I wondered, *"Did anyone receive Christ or have a miracle?"***

About four days later a man called me from about 1200 miles away (about 2000 kilometers) and said, *"I can't get your name out of my mind."* (An attorney I knew had told him about me and the Lord kept bringing my name to his mind.) He asked me, *"Do you need anything?"* I answered him. **"I don't need anything; Jesus Christ takes care of all my needs!"**

He said *"Well, I want to do something for you anyway. Can you meet me tomorrow at the South Coast Plaza?"* I told him I would and the next day he took me shopping for clothes. Every time he would give me a $100 travelers cheque I would tithe out of it. He said, *"You don't have to tithe out of that; I've already tithed. That's you money to spend."* I told him, *"That's O.K. I know Who blesses me and I'm going to tithe to God."*

I walked out of that shopping center with eight (8) changes of clothes and a new pair of handsome kidskin shoes!

I DIED to the rain (to my one suit and one pair of dress shoes) ... and God brought resurrection: eight changes of clothing!! There was an important reason God wanted me to go preach, even if I didn't SEE it that day.

Another time when God asked me to go preach in a heavy rainstorm, I didn't SEE anything happen at the time. However, in **a few days a lady called me** (I don't know how she obtained my phone number) and said, *"You don't know who I am, but I was driving down Broadway and saw you preaching in the rain. **My husband is blind and he was with me in the car.** I described you to him and he said, 'I would like to meet that man.'"* She was amazed because she told me, *"My* *husband doesn't want anything to do with preachers."* She said, *"Could we meet you somewhere?"* [Note: the lady had mentioned seeing me preaching in the rain to a friend in her city who miraculously knew who I was (when the lady described me) and knew my phone number.]

I felt the Lord impressing me to invite them to my home for dinner. When they came to dinner, the Lord allowed me to **lead the man to Christ.** About six months later I heard a loud knock on my door. It was the lady's husband. He came in and hugged me and told me that about two weeks before he had been **baptized in the Holy Spirit, and healed so that he could now see!**

I died to the rain … and God brought resurrection power.

What is God asking YOU to DIE TO? Is it that power play in your family or at the office, is it your impatience or your ego, OR is it that interpersonal relationship at your synagogue, your church or your ministry? What is it about which the Lord is … or has been … dealing with you? Is it a person or thing? I promise you on the authority of God's Holy Word that if YOU will DIE to that, God will bring forth resurrection life!

Remember, the Holy Spirit is God's agent on earth to supply the resurrection power of Christ!

Pray NOW … obey God, and yield to Him. Die to that situation, person, or thing … and then watch God bring resurrection life and multiply it around the world!

16

EXPERIENCE RESURRECTION
DIE TO COMFORT ZONES

Jesus taught, *"Except a grain of wheat falls into the ground and die, it abides alone: but if it die, it brings forth much fruit."* [John 12:24]

What is it that God is asking YOU to DIE TO at this point of your life and ministry?

If YOU will DIE to that thing, or to those things, about which God is speaking TO YOU, you will see increased productivity: resurrection power!

In 1976 I and my family of five lived in a little 22 foot by 22-foot house. There was one bedroom and I even disposed of the bed so I could use the bedroom for an office (volunteer workers would come over and work in the other part of the house).

My family and I were sleeping on the floor at night. The children were little and sometimes they would wet the bed (the floor!) while sleeping. I decided I was going to do something about this. That is, **let God do something about it!**

After praying, the Lord laid it upon my heart to give a certain portion (offering) above my tithe to Him for six (6) months. **The offering amount was a very high portion: higher than I had ever given**. During those months I would get up before dawn and write down Bible verses on cards, then memorize them and record them onto cassettes. **I DIED to both the comfort of sleep and the comfort of only giving my usual offering amount above the tithe.**

At the end of the six months I was instructed of the Lord to leave that place (I really liked it - **it was my comfort zone**) and take my family with me to another state far away. When I arrived there, I located my family in a nice place to stay and decided to get alone for a while in a previously used animal shed on a farm in a rural area.

I locked myself into the shed and instructed that no one should come see me or contact me because I wanted to fast and be alone with the Lord. **I took in enough water to last for 40 days**. I shut myself in, making sure the door and all windows were locked and covered, making it impossible for anyone to come in or to see in.

After a few days I heard footsteps approaching the shed in the barn. I had instructed my family that nobody was to come there or to try to contact me. **I just wanted to be alone with God.** When I heard the footsteps I even placed a chair against the door (even though it was locked) to make sure nobody could enter. Then, I heard the footsteps walk away; there was no knock and no voice.

Later, I looked under the chair and saw an envelope. **When I opened it I found $75,000 USD**. I didn't know what to do … except praise God!!! **I stayed another few days and the same thing happened, only this time there was $25,000 USD. That made a total of $100,000 dollars US!** I talked to God about it: I said, *"God, I know I promised you I would be with here for 40 days, but I think I need to go to the bank!"*

No, I did NOT sell my soul. Actually, God understood and used this money to keep me from serious damage to my body. The animal shed where I was fasting had just been painted before I locked myself in, and I would have been seriously injured internally (poisoned) had I stayed there longer. **God not only used the money to bless me, but also to get me out of the place to protect my body from harm**. As it was, I had some bad effects later from just the few days I was there.

I died to my comfort zone of a home where I was reaching nations and where I had lived for a few years: where people knew me and where the ministry was centered; and **God brought resurrection power – increased productivity - to many nations, tribes, and peoples!**

I was able to purchase printing equipment that helped me reach many more thousands of people in many languages, and to travel overseas to nations with the Good News! **Many new churches have been raised up through the literature we have published through the years.**

People still listen to programs and podcasts that have were made possible by the $100,000 MIRACLE described above.

We purchased time and put these programs on in major market radio stations for 40 consecutive broadcasts—eight weeks, five times a week, Monday through Friday—and offered $36 in FREE Bible teaching cassettes to anyone who would write. These messages have been duplicated around the world in the last 37 years and ended up in far away villages in other countries; and eventually led us into podcasting (which I release all over the world right now).

Miracles - real miracles - were experienced by people as they listened to these broadcasts. One man wrote us and said as he was driving down the highway **he put his hand on the radio and it felt like electricity was going through his body as he was instantly healed**.

What is God asking YOU to DIE TO? Is it that power play down at the office, is it your impatience or your ego, OR is it that interpersonal relationship at your church or ministry?

What is it about which the Lord is or has been dealing with you? Is it a person or thing? I promise you on the authority of God's Holy Word that if YOU will DIE to that person or thing, God will bring forth resurrection life!

Pray NOW ... obey God, and yield to Him. **Die to that situation, person, or thing ... and then watch God bring resurrection life - increased productivity - and multiply it around the world!**

Remember, the Holy Spirit is God's agent on earth to supply the resurrection power of Christ!

I know this teaching will help you experience miracles, increased productivity, and resurrection power.

EXPERIENCE RESURRECTION
DIE TO AUTOMOBILES

Jesus taught, *"Except a grain of wheat falls into the ground and die, it abides alone: but if it die, it brings forth much fruit."*(John 12:24)

What is it that God is asking YOU to DIE TO at this point of your life, business, or ministry?

If YOU will DIE to that thing, or to those things, about which God is speaking TO YOU, you will see resurrection!

There is a place where I used to go and write for months. It was a 200-acre farm, and one time I was there during harvest season. I helped take in the harvest, shoveling corn in the large corn cribs as it was brought in from the fields. There was an average of three ears of corn on every shock in the field. We counted the grains of corn on one ear. **From one grain of corn, which was planted and DIED, a harvest of 1,800 grains came back.**

One time at a Christian retreat in the mountains I was delivering an exegesis of the passage in Romans 6:15-23, specifically on *"Fruit unto Holiness."* I used the example above about the planting and death of seeds. After the session, a man came to me and said to me: *"I grow cantaloupe (melons). Every seed I plant which dies produces six melons, and **each melon has an*** *average of 300 seeds. This gives me a return of 1,800 seeds."*

What is it that God is asking YOU to DIE TO at this point of your life, business, or ministry?

If YOU will DIE to that thing, or to those things, about which God is speaking TO YOU, you will see resurrection!

In the parable of the sower (Mark 4:1-9), Jesus taught that the seed which is planted in good ground brings forth fruit some thirty fold, some sixty, and some a hundred. **Note: "one hundredfold" equals "10,000 percent"!** Jesus taught, *"Except a grain of wheat falls into the ground and die, it abides alone: **but if it die, it brings forth much fruit**."* (John 12:24)

One time God told me to give my car away to a preacher. I did NOT want to do it; I had already given a car to a preacher and God had blessed me back. However, I kept feeling that God wanted me to give the car to the man of God. I thought of a way to obey, but which legally before God might keep me from having to give the car away! (How foolish! Can we trick God?)

I thought: *"I will call the man about midnight (he lived in another county about 30 to 45 minutes away). I will ask him to come to my home right away, and tell him that I need to talk to him about something. If he doesn't come, then I will NOT have to give my car away!"*

When I called the man near midnight, he answered and said, *"I will be right over."* He did NOT know what I wanted (or did NOT want) to tell him. I thought, *"I better get on my knees and pray. I have about 30 minutes to get in the right frame of heart (or, attitude) whereby I can give this automobile away with a WILLING, cheerful, heart!"* After about 28 minutes I came to the place where I could give the car away cheerfully. And I did so when he came a few minutes later.

Through the years I have given several automobiles away to preachers. So far, God has blessed me back with so many automobiles I have lost count. Some of them were the finest and most expensive cars made in the USA. **You can NEVER out give God!**

I DIED to my cars and God brought resurrection!

What is God asking YOU to DIE TO? Is it that power play down at the office, is it your impatience or your ego, OR is it that interpersonal relationship at your synagogue or church?

What is it about which the Lord is - or has been - dealing with you? Is it a person or thing? God will never deny you anything - or anyone - except to give you something else, or someone else, better!

I promise you on the authority of God's Holy Word that if YOU will DIE to that situation about which God is dealing with you, God will bring forth resurrection life!

Pray NOW. Obey God, and yield to Him. Die to that situation, person, or thing, and then watch God bring resurrection life - increased productivity - and multiply it around the world!

EXPERIENCE RESURRECTION
DIE TO MINISTRY

Yeshua (Jesus) taught, *"Except a grain of wheat falls into the ground and die, it abides alone: but if it die, it brings forth much fruit."* (John 12:24)

What is it that God is asking YOU to DIE TO at this point of your life and ministry?

If YOU will DIE to that thing, or to those things, about which God is speaking TO YOU, you will see resurrection!

Unfed sheep will scatter. Today we see many large churches and synagogues. **Does this mean the sheep are being fed**, or does it mean they are being fed, but possibly NOT being fed nutritious food, just junk spiritual food. Lots of restaurants cater to large crowds (especially on Sundays) but does that mean the food is nutritious? Large synagogues and churches are NOT necessarily a sign of productive ministry in the eyes of the LORD.

To be a productive synagogue or church (in the eyes of the LORD) the rabbi or shepherd–leader must be obedient: **He / she must attempt to create, or to form, a RESURRECTION synagogue or church: a real New Covenant synagogue or church**. Programs and cell groups mean nothing if people are not being instructed in the ministry precepts of Jesus. WHAT are those precepts? **Look at what Jesus instructed His followers to do** in Mark 3:14-15:

> Preach and teach;

> Heal the sick; and

> Cast out demons.

Also, **look at the Great Commission**:

> *"And Jesus came and spake unto them, saying, All power is given unto me in heaven and in earth.*

> *Go ye therefore, and **teach all nations**, **baptizing them** in the name of the Father, and of the Son, and of the Holy Ghost:*

> ***Teaching them to observe all things whatsoever I have commanded you**: and, lo, I am with you alway, even unto the end of the world. Amen."* (Matthew 28:18-20)

What are some of the things Jesus taught and commanded us? Here are a few: love, prayer, faith, healing, discipleship, casting out demons, forgiveness, binding and loosing, etc.

Rabbis and pastors that do NOT minister healing are cheating the flock over which God has placed them. Why do they do this? Usually because they do NOT believe in healing. Oh, they will tell you, *"I believe*

Jesus can heal," or, *"we have had people healed,"* but the TRUTH is they do NOT know **HOW** to minister healing so they dismiss it. That is, **they either do NOT believe Jesus WILL heal, or they do NOT have the faith to pray or believe for healing**. The same applies to MIRACLES: real miracles!

God told Ezekiel to prophesy to the shepherds of **the flock of God**: *"The diseased have ye not strengthened, neither have ye healed that which was sick, neither have ye bound up that which was broken, neither have ye brought again that which was driven away, neither have ye sought that which was lost."*

Many times rabbis and pastors look upon **their congregation** as **their flock**, when in reality they are **the flock of God**; also, there are **many outside who are in the flock of God** but can NOT receive ministry. For example, they may need healing (including some in the flock of parishioners) but do NOT receive healing because it is NOT being ministered, or served, in the church local to them.

Healing ministry should be a part of all church worship services, or at least one service a week designated for healing (and the people informed of the time and location.) But what about people who are sick, diseased, bound, or afflicted who come to ANY service in need of healing, deliverance, or prayer?

The same applies to the Baptism in the Holy Spirit and instruction concerning it.

Let me ask you some questions:

When - or how often - **does your synagogue or church pray for sick people and lay hands on them**? How often are people anointed with oil (either in meetings or in their homes)?

When - or how often - **are people being sent out (commissioned / ordained) to the service of God** with the laying on of hands?

When - or how often - **are people baptized in the Holy Spirit (and speak in tongues) for the first time** in your synagogue or church?

A person said to me the other day, *"Healing is for salvation: to bring people to Christ."* I answered them, *"Healing is **part** of salvation; PART of the WHOLENESS of Christ. So is the Baptism in the Holy Spirit, deliverance, prosperity, ministry, and Kingdom responsibility."* Healing is for the sick to be healed. **One miracle healing can do more than 25 years of preaching.**

Salvation is wholeness. The Hebrew word commonly used for salvation in the Old Testament is **Yeshua** (the name of Jesus) and means: **deliverance, health, victory, prosperity, welfare**. In the New Testament it is the Greek word **soteria** and means **rescue or safety (physically or morally), deliver, health, save**. If pastors / shepherds were doing their job, they would **include and offer ALL of salvation**. Then mass

29

numbers would come to Christ. The church would be the church.

Just recently a person told me, *"I believe in keeping the ramp down low to make it easy for people to come to Christ."* This is foolishness, because Jesus made it possible for there to be an infinite number of approaches to Him. God said, *"Whosoever."* However, having the ramp down low, or whatever angle, **must include repentance**. When a person comes to Christ, there should be a CHANGE in their lifestyle: in any lifestyle, no matter what ramp they took to Jesus. *"Repent, and be baptized every one of you in the name of Yeshua HaMashiach (Jesus the Christ) for the remission of sins, and ye shall receive the gift of the Holy Ghost. For the promise is unto you, and to your children, and to all that are afar off, even as many as the Lord our God shall call."* (Acts 2:38-39)

In years past I attended churches where there were numbers of people coming to Messiah Jesus, where healings, miracles, baptisms in the Spirit, deliverances, and great teachings were always present. **I taught at a graduate theological seminary where one Thursday morning prayer meeting (in the founding church) so many miracles happened that 77 people were baptized in water.** Thousands were turned away at the doors at special meetings.

➡ I saw a lady devastated with cancer, get up out of her wheel chair in church healed, and her slip—her under garment—fell off because she was so skinny.

30

➡ I saw a man with his head locked into his wheel chair (because part of his spinal column was removed)— his nurse took him to church—get up out of his wheel chair completely healed and walk after the nurse unlocked his head. These are only a couple of the MANY healings and miracles I could write about.

➡ I have seen blind eyes opened, deaf ears unstopped, people walking out of wheel chairs, demons cast out—all part of the **NORMAL** SYNAGOGUE AND CHURCH MINISTRY.

There are many good expositors today, but NOT many good teachers. WHY? **Because only PART of salvation (wholeness) is taught**. It has been my experience in the past that whenever the WHOLENESS of Christ is preached, the teaching will be dynamic, edifying, prophetic, and gift accompanied. **A truly gifted teacher (one who has the ministry gift of teaching) will see and experience the gifts of the Spirit (which include healing and prophecy and tongues) accompany the ministry of the Word**. The Holy Spirit will always defer to the Word of God where there is faith and expectancy to go along with it. And, usually faith and expectancy will go along with the Word, because *"faith comes by hearing, and hearing by the Word of God."*

Many synagogues and churches see people coming to Messiah with lots of Bible studies and home prayer and cell groups; however, **MANY MORE could be saved if the rabbis and pastors–shepherds would have the**

boldness, the faith, and the compassion to minister the WHOLENESS of Messiah Jesus.

Let me say to you today, my brother or sister in the LORD, if you are a rabbi or pastor–shepherd and you are NOT providing your people with the WHOLENESS of Messiah, the complete Good News, **when you stand before Jesus, He will ask you,** *"Why did you cheat my people?"*

It's like a party of blind men, none of which will tell the others they are blind. They all see nothing, **but act as though they do see**. No healing service offered for the sick or afflicted, no ministry related to the importance of praying in tongues, no deliverance for the mentally, physically or spiritually oppressed (or possessed). And many times **justified by theology** that teaches these things stopped happening after the early synagogue– church. In other words, the real Jesus is partially paralyzed. He is NOT the same today as He was, even though the scripture teaches: *"Jesus Christ the same yesterday, and to day, and for ever."* (Hebrews 13:8)

Just as the lawyers and Pharisees rejected the counsel of God not receiving the baptism of John, likewise many rabbis and pastor–shepherd—and trained theologians—today reject the counsel of God by not receiving the Baptism in the Holy Spirit, **justifying their actions, or inactions, on the overt basis of theology or their church doctrine, or the covert basis of pride and fear of persecution.** *"They are (as Jesus described) like unto children sitting in the marketplace, and calling one to another, and saying, We have piped*

32

unto you, and ye have not danced; we have mourned to you, and ye have not wept."

And the sad thing is that many of these rabbis and shepherds once operated in the gifts of the Spirit, and have turned their backs on them **for reasons that have earned them the sterility and impotency** they are experiencing. *"Pleasers of men, but not of God."*

Look at the New Testament Synagogue or Church in the Book of Acts. Look at your flock (whether you are the rabbi or pastor–shepherd or a member of the congregation). If you are the rabbi or pastor–shepherd, you can at least do your part: preach and teach WHAT Jesus told you to; and minister the WHOLENESS of Christ. **At least do your part: TRY!**

WARNING: You will have to pay the price of being ostracized, persecuted, and maligned by people and the devil. However, you will be BLESSED by the LORD.

CHALLENGE: Take some time alone in prayer and fasting, and make a commitment to minister the WHOLENESS of Messiah Jesus. He is willing to help you in this consecration. If you do NOT have the faith to believe in His wholeness, or if you do NOT believe Jesus the Messiah is the same today as He was in the past, **ask Him to forgive you, and then ask Him to help your unbelief**.

EXPERIENCE RESURRECTION
DIE TO REASONING

IMPLEMENT NEW IDEAS

Yeshua (Jesus) taught, *"Except a grain of wheat falls into the ground and die, it abides alone: but if it die, it brings forth much fruit."* (John 12:24)

What is it that God is asking YOU to DIE TO at this point of your life and ministry?

If YOU will DIE to that thing, or to those things, about which God is speaking TO YOU, you will see resurrection!

When God gives you a **NEW IDEA**, the devil will tell you, *"That is not reasonable; that is NOT wise. You shouldn't do that."*

God wants you to be willing to respond to Him when He tells you to do something. **If you'll just give God the benefit of the doubt—and die to your reasoning—you'll start seeing more MIRACLES than ever before!**

Learn to listen, and to obey, God in the little things as well as the big things!

Die to reasoning and let God GROW the NEW IDEA He gives you. Give Him the benefit of the doubt, and you will SEE **resurrection of accomplishment** in your purposes, your life, your business, your family, and your ministry!

There are certain limits to your abilities. However, if you will die to reasoning and listen to the voice of the Holy Spirit, you will be able to accomplish things:

> Your mind has never conceived.

> That people (even yourself) have said are impossible.

> That the enemy (the devil) has said, You cannot do this!

Remember, the scripture says, *"The things that are impossible with men are possible with God."* (Luke 18:27)

➡ I am aware by the Spirit of God that someone who is reading this book has **an IDEA God has given you**; however, you either:

> Do not know HOW to accomplish it (you need wisdom from God); or,

> You are not POSITIVE the idea came from God.

MY ADVICE TO YOU:

First, the enemy of your soul will always lie to your mind if have an IDEA, or are working on an idea, to reach people and nations for the Messiah of Israel.

Second, do NOT share your vision with others unless they are people who are involved directly in creative works of God. Read the examples below to encourage you.

EXAMPLE 1 - On one website search of like subject matter, out of over 63,000,000 (that's million) like subjects, we were #1. Also, there were several sites where we were #1 out of tens of thousands. I give ALL the credit to the Holy Spirit (Ruach HaKodesh). I **turned down every piece of advice I received from media people directly involved with that industry**. Some were friends. Some were experts with top credentials and experience in the field.

ASK GOD FOR WISDOM & DO WHAT HE TELLS YOU!

EXAMPLE 2 - On one project that has **reached some of the wealthiest Jews in the world and hundreds of thousands of people for the Messiah of Israel**, I was told by a government agency that I could NOT do it: that it violated laws, codes, and restrictions five (5) different ways.

ASK GOD FOR WISDOM & DO NOT TAKE "NO" FOR AN ANSWER!

EXAMPLE 3 - On one project the Lord gave me to do which has reached hundreds of thousands, if not millions, for Christ in many languages around the world, I was seeking feedback. I wanted the opinion, or advice, from someone. It was a far out IDEA and so I thought of the most far out person I was acquainted with to see what they thought of the IDEA. The **person told me, It is too far out for me!** That was my sign the idea was from God.

ASK GOD FOR WISDOM & DON'T LISTEN TO OTHER PEOPLE!

EXAMPLE 4 - Before I went on one ministry trip, a good close brother in the Lord told me, You are NOT supposed to go on that trip. However, I decided to do what God told me and I went on the trip. By God's grace I reached many for Messiah Yeshua. Jews were saved, and God crossed my path with a person who had information they passed on to me before they died which helped me reach many, many Jews in Israel and around the world!

ASK GOD FOR WISDOM & FINISH THE JOB!

EXAMPLE 5 - One project the Lord let me be part of - I actually only WATCHED Him put it together - took only one day! **All came together in one day: the IDEA, the money, the machines, the methodology, and the people.** I really had nothing to do with it except ride around with a lady in a Jaguar and go from step to step as the Holy Spirit directed. Tens of thousands of Jews, if not more, around the world (many in Israel), have been reached for Messiah.

One Jewish businessman from Tiberius, Israel, flew all the way to California to meet me. I had an unlisted phone number; I don't know how he found my number. He told me, I will pay anything to meet you. I met him and spent two hours in the Tanakh (the Hebrew Scriptures). The Ruach HaKodesh (the Holy Spirit) opened his spiritual eyes; the man prayed and asked Yeshua HaMashiach (Jesus the Messiah) to come into his life and be his Messiah. I then took him to the airline counter where he immediately booked a flight back to Israel.

ASK GOD FOR WISDOM & MOVE EXPEDITIOUSLY!

If Christopher Columbus had looked at the horizon from the ocean shore and listened to many others he would never have sailed to the New World 500 years ago.

What is YOUR horizon?

What is that stirring in your heart God has been activating? What is that IDEA the Lord has given you that you feel is humanly impossible?

ASK GOD FOR WISDOM

DIE TO REASONING

GOD WILL BRING RESURRECTION

PLUS CREATIVITY IN THE SPIRIT

ADDENDUM

One time God told me to go to a large metropolitan area and **preach in the open air from about 10 PM until midnight**. As I was preaching, I thought, *"There's nobody here to even hear me. Why did God send me here?"* However, I kept preaching in faith.

A little while later a young man told me that across the street from where I was preaching the military would house young men waiting to go to the military the next day. They would place them there for one more day of medical checks before being shipped off to basic training. I returned to that area again - and sure enough - **several stories up there were young men listening out the windows** on their way to the Army the next day.

About six months later I was invited to a party in Hollywood. I thought, *"I can go witness for my Lord."* There were so many people at that home that it was literally hard to move or walk around. I found myself standing opposite to a young man with red hair. He asked me what I did and I told him I was a minister.

He told me that he was the son of a Southern Baptist pastor, but that he, himself, had never received Christ. He then told me something very interesting. He said that one night he was **in the hotel across the street from where God had sent me to preach in the late night**. He said that at night, while listening to the preaching, **he wrestled with Satan for hours until he**

finally got on his knees and gave his life to the Lord Jesus. He was saved and eternally thankful for the preaching that came to him in the nighttime.

I DIED to my reasoning and God brought forth resurrection life!

Do what the Holy Spirit tells you. You may have a sense of the limits of your abilities but remember, *"With man it is impossible, but with God ALL things are possible."*

I know this teaching will help you to be super productive in the Kingdom.

Have a wonderful life serving God and may His grace abound more and more as you progress on your journey to Heaven, showing other people the Way. Here's a promise for YOU. I have seen many MIRACLES claiming this promise from GOD:

"Call to me and I will answer you, and show you great and mighty things which you do not know."
– Tanakh: Jeremiah 33:3

LIVE A LIFE OF EXCELLENCE!

OTHER BOOKS BY PRINCE HANDLEY

- Map of the End Times
- How to Do Great Works
- Flow Chart of Revelation
- Action Keys for Success
- Health and Healing Complete Guide to Wholeness
- Prophetic Calendar for Israel & the Nations: Thru 2023
- Healing Deliverance
- How to Receive God's Power with Gifts of the Spirit
- Healing for Mental and Physical Abuse
- Victory Over Opposition and Resistance
- Healing of Emotional Wounds
- How to Be Healed and Live in Divine Health
- Healing from Fear, Shame and Anger
- How to Receive Healing and Bring Healing to Others
- New Global Strategy: Enabling Missions
- The Art of Christian Warfare
- Success Cycles and Secrets
- New Testament Bible Studies (A Study Manual)
- Babylon the Bitch: Enemy of Israel
- Resurrection Multiplication – Miracle Production
- Faith and Quantum Physics – Create Your Future
- Conflict Healing – Relational Health
- Decision Making 101 – Know for Sure

AVAILABLE AT AMAZON AND OTHER BOOK STORES

UNIVERSITY OF EXCELLENCE PRESS
Los Angeles ■ London ■ Tel Aviv

BONUS

To help you, and to help you teach others, we have prepared Rabbinical Studies at this site:

www.uofe.org/RABBINICAL_STUDIES.html

These are commentaries from **ancient** Jewish Rabbis that identify the Mashiach of Israel.

To help you, and to help you teach others, we have also prepared Bible Studies from the Brit Chadashah (the New Testament) in English, Spanish and French.

- English FREE Bible Studies
  www.uofe.org/english_bible_studies.html
- Spanish FREE Bible Studies
  www.uofe.org/spanish_bible_studies.html
- French FREE Bible Studies
  www.uofe.org/french_bible_studies.html

ANNOUNCEMENT

We recommend you obtain the companion books to this book:

Action Keys for Success

Success Cycles and Secrets

How to Do Great Works

Victory Over Opposition and Resistance

All four books are available at Amazon and other good book stores.

Prince Handley Books
marketplaceworld.com

⊥

NOTE

We listen to our readers. Tell us what **new** subject matter you would like to see published. Email your ideas to: universityofexcellence@gmail.com.

www.ingramcontent.com/pod-product-compliance
Lightning Source LLC
Chambersburg PA
CBHW060634030426
42337CB00018B/3352